Eugenio

D0978290

Pompeii

new practical guide

*3 recommended itineraries and
map for touring the excavations
Useful information*

BONECHI EDIZIONI "IL TURISMO" FIRENZE

Exclusive distributor for Naples and the Campania Region:
VERBEL & C. S.a.s.
di Mariarosaria Bello
via Domenico Quaranta, 23
80126 NAPOLI (Loggetta)
Tel. 081/59.39.446

© Copyright 1999 by Bonechi Edizioni "Il Turismo" S.r.l.
Via dei Rustici, 5 - 50122 FLORENCE
Tel. +39 055.239.82.24/25
Fax +39 055.21.63.66
E-mail: barbara@bonechi.com
        bbonechi@dada.it
http://www.bonechi.com

Photographs: Bonechi Edizioni "Il Turismo" S.r.l. archives
Photographs: Studio Fotografico Mimmo Jodice: page 3 - 20 - 21 - 33
        (on top) - 39 (at the bottom) - 45 - 78 - 81 - 110 - 111
Translated by: Julia Weiss
Layout, cover, maps and illustration pages 6-7: Lorenzo Cerrina
Edited by: Lorena Lazzari
Photolithography: Fotolito Immagine, Florence
Printed by: La Zincografica Fiorentina, Florence
ISBN 88-7204-374-3

Mount Somma and Vesuvius, seen from the sea.

Welcome to Pompeii

Before you start on your walk through the glorious ruins of Pompeii to take one of the most incredible journeys into the past, I would like to welcome you, and thank you for having come here, perhaps even from distant cities and countries.

Visiting this so-called "dead city", the city that has been unearthed, may arouse feelings of sorrow and religious respect. However, beyond all expectations, as you follow this guidebook step by step you will realize that the city is actually alive and filled with pleasant surprises even though from time you time it will remind you of its tragedy.

We have tried to make your visit easy, and to render the excavations as comprehensible as possible, down to the smallest detail. This applies especially to archeological terminology and the differences in painting and architectural styles.

We hope that we have succeeded in our goal of making you participate in the city's daily life by describing various customs and habits and telling you about people who, though separated from us by nearly two millennia, were actually not all that different from us today.

The Publisher

SUGGESTIONS FOR TOURING THE EXCAVATIONS

The itinerary is shown on the topographic map of the excavations, numbered from 1 to 57. If you follow it you will see all the excavations. However this requires a great deal of time since seeing just the excavations within the perimetral walls of the uncovered city requires over five hours. Then there is the Villa of the Mysteries which can be reached by car or horse-drawn carriage. For those whose time is limited we suggest three itineraries and the numbers to follow as they are shown on the

FIRST ITINERARY
(one and a half hours)

n. 1, 2, 3, 4, 5, 8, 12, 13, 14, 15, 21, 22, 23

SECOND ITINERARY
(two and a half hours)

n. 1, 3, 4, 5, 8, 9, 10, 11, 12, 13, 14, 15, 21, 22, 23, 33, 38, 40, 41

THIRD ITINERARY
(three and a half hours)

n. 1, 2, 4, 5, 8, 9, 10, 11, 12, 13, 14, 15, 21, 23, 33, 38, 40, 41, 42, 43, 44, 46, 47, 48, 49, 50, 51, 52, 53, 54

THE HISTORY OF THE ANCIENT CITY

No one knows the exact origins of ancient Pompeii. Even its name is uncertain, since no one has been able to determine whether it is Greek or Italic. However, the version accepted by most scholars is that it may come from the Greek "pémpo, pompé" or from the Oscan "pomp", since the city was probably founded by the Oscans who dominated the Campania region. What is known for certain dates from the VI century B.C. because the city was already active with its first urban center surrounded by a solid circle of walls. However, there is no doubt that it probably existed as early as the VIII century B.C., perhaps as a limited nucleus of farmers with dwellings scattered in the Sarno valley. The basis for this is its geographic position, it rises on a plateau and overlooks the plain where the river flows to the sea providing a harbor for the daring Phoenician and Greek navigators who wanted to increase their trade. It was mainly the Greeks who had settled at Cumae and took over the entire Gulf of Naples as far as Sorrento, Capri and Ischia who first looked at Pompeii. The opportunity of bringing it into the orbit of the power Cumano state came from the hostility of the Etruscans who dominated the Campania hinterland. In order to survive Pompeii was forced to ally itself politically and commercially with the Greeks of Cumae. The Etruscans, however, did not ignore this event and regained the positions they had lost between 525 and 474 B.C. They only ruled a short time because their fleet was defeated by the Greeks and the city once again came under the victors' hegemony. The Pompeians were not sufficiently organized to defend themselves against the Etruscans and the Greeks, therefore they could not hope to live independently. In fact, when in the V century B.C. the Samnites from Hirpinia and Samnium defeated the Greeks and Etruscans, Pompeii was forced to submit to new masters. From that time on the city was governed according to Samnite laws and customs which it absorbed with the language and religion. Little is known about the city's life during the Samnite domination, however it could not have been tranquil for in the year 310 B.C. the Pompeians and Nucerians were forced to take arms to defend themselves against the raids of the Roman fleet that landed its men at the mouth of the Sarno river and looted the coast. The by now powerful Rome defeated the Samnites and Pompeii had to accept a special form of "association" that allowed a certain amount of independence. However, during the period of the Social War launched by the Italians against Rome, the city

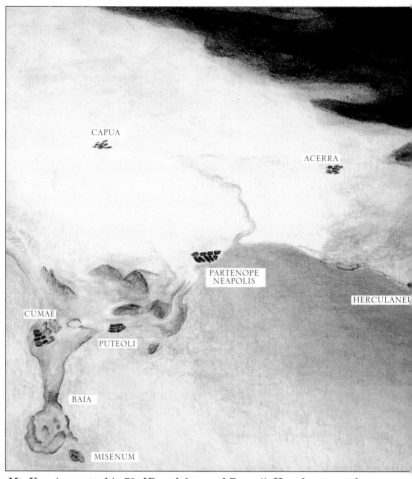

Mt. Vesuvius erupted in 79 AD and destroyed Pompeii, Herculaneum and Stabia (reconstruction by Lorenzo Cerrina).

decided to shake the yoke and fight for its freedom. After several vicissitudes Rome defeated the Italians at Nola and Pompeii officially became a colony, Colonia Cornelia Veneria in 80 B.C. It was not easy for Rome to subdue so many political, economic and social differences, but with time the Pompeians became so completely Roman as to accept the language, customs, laws and munici-pal ordinances.

Tacitus says something of the Pompeian character in the *Annals* as he tells of the tragic and terrible brawl that broke out between the Pompeians and Nucerians during a gladiatorial spectacle in the Amphitheater. It was the year 59 B.C. and four gladiators, two local men and two from Nuceria, were fighting in the arena. Their skills drove the crowd of spectators

mad, and as at all sporting events they were cheering for their favorites. Evidently one local fan made some nasty comment about the other team and the fight deteriorated into a brawl and then into the slaughter of as many Nucerians as the Pompeians could get their hands on. The fact was relayed to Rome and Nero explained it to the Senate and this resulted in the amphitheater being closed for ten years. The first sign of the tragedy that was to strike Pompeii came from the terrible earthquake of 62 A.D. The city, like many others in the region, suffered severe damages. When the fear of another quake had passed reconstruction and restoration of the temples, and public and private buildings began. The city built new luxurious homes, workshops and stores, increasing its econo-

AERIAL VIEW OF THE FORUM AND THE MAIN MONUMENTS

A) *Aediles*	**TV)** *Temple of Vespasian*
B) *Basilica*	**1)** *Tribunal of the Basilica*
C) *Curia*	**2)** *Entrance portico to the Basilica*
D) *Duumviri*	**3)** *Portico of the Samnite Forum*
E) *Building of Eumachia*	**4, 5,** *Statues of Claudius, Augustus,*
M) *Macellum*	**6, 7)** *Agrippina, Nero*
T) *Baths*	**8)** *Comitium*
TA) *Temple of Apollo*	**9)** *Portico of the Roman Forum*
TC) *Temple of Augusto*	**10)** *Podium for auctions*
TG) *Temple of Jupiter*	**11)** *Apse of the Building of Eumachia*
TL) *Sanctuary of the Lares*	**12)** *Statue of the Priestess Eumachia*

mic, commercial and industrial strength. However, seventeen years later on 24 August 79 A.D., slightly after twelve o'clock noon the incredible disaster struck. Vesuvius erupted literally burying the city (along with Herculaneum and Stabia) under six to seven meters of ash, lapilli and volanic matter. Only a few managed to escape. Most of the population that numbered around twenty thousand died of suffocation in the streets, houses and cellars where many thought they could find refuge from the destructive fury of the fire and poisonous gases. Chilling evidence of this agony can be seen in the plaster casts made from the cavities left by human bodies enclosed in the hard shell of ash and lapilli. The fleet based at Misenum came to help the Pompeians, led by Pliny the Elder who, in addition to being an admiral was an outstanding scholar of natural phenomena. However, not even he could do anything: his noble humanitarian and scientific efforts led to his death. What we do know about the eruption comes from his nephew, Pliny the Younger in two dramatic letters he sent to Tacitus. As time passed and the volcano continued to erupt nothing more was known about Pompeii to the extent that, notwithstanding Pliny's letters, no one could even discover the exact location of the city. Even when the architect Domenico Fontana was excavating a canal (from 1594 to 1600) to carry water from the Sarno to Torre Annunziata and discovered ruins and inscriptions, he did not realize that he had actually found Pompeii. In 1748 the Bourbon king, Charles began the first excavations, however, they were little more than shafts sunken into the ground to remove objects and statues from the homes. A major impetus came during the Napoleonic period, then between 1815 and 1832 the Forum, the Basilica, the House of the Faun, the houses of the Tragic Poet, of Pansa and the Forum Baths were discovered; the Stabian baths were brought to light between 1850-59. When the Kingdom of Italy was established the excavations were entrusted to Giuseppe Fiorelli in 1860. He began work using a scientific method. It is to him that we owe the brilliant idea of making casts of the hollows left in the hardened ash by the disintegrated bodies of the victims and various wood items. Fiorelli was followed by distinguished archeologists who perfected the excavation methods such as Michele Ruggiero, Giulio De Petra, Antonio Sogliano and Vittorio Pinazzola. The person who did the most, however, by bringing to light three fifths of the city's area was the late archeologist, Professor Amedeo Maiuri who worked in Pompeii from 1924 to 1962. Those who wish to learn more about the secrets of archeological excavations in Campania can read his numerous essays and books.

THE URBAN STRUCTURE OF THE CITY

The removal of the thick blanket of ash and lapilli uncovered an unusual urbanistic structure, that cannot be found in any other Roman city, to the astonished eyes of archeologists and posterity. Pompeii, as we said in the historic notes, had been dominated by various other peoples: Etruscans, Greeks, Samnites and Romans as well as the primitive Italic people who certainly built the first urban nucleus where we can now see the Forum. The city thus had various urbanistic experiences all of which are recognizable because of the construction techniques and materials used by the different rulers. Thus, five construction epochs have been identified: the pre-Samnite from the VI to V century B.C., the Samnite from the IV to III century B.C., the second Samnite period that was influenced by the Hellenistic culture, from 200-80 B.C., the first Roman Period (80 B.C. to 14 A.D.), that was Republican and Augustan and

Aerial view of the excavations in Pompeii

the second Roman period (14-79 A.D.) that included the Claudian and Flavian eras. Each of these epochs had its own construction methods using different materials according to experiences acquired over the years. From this scholars have been able to ascertain the various phases in the transformation of the city and its buildings. Naturally, the greatest imprint was left by the Romans of the Republican and Imperial eras. But, contrary to what is the prototype of the "square" city according to the dictates of urban Quirites, here it was the unusual configuration of the land itself that caused the city to be built on a bed of prehistoric lava nearly 40 meters above sea level. This forced the planners to work according to the terrain which slopes not insignificantly from north to south, while the flat part is located at the western end of the city. It is precisely in this flat part that the most important public buildings are located, while the true center is filled with an agglomerate of houses arranged in blocks forming straight streets that intersect at right angles and are flanked by narrow sidewalks. At the intersections there are fountains, and along the streets there are large stones to make it easier for pedestrians to cross. At the two ends of the residential area are the Triangular Forum and theaters to the south, and while the large amphitheater and palestra (gymnasium) are to the south east. The fortified walls are 3.220 kilometers long and the inhabited part of the city extends over 66 hectares. One of the most lively features of the city are the inscriptions. They can be considered a true accessory of city life. As the excavations proceeded it became necessary to collect and decipher these inscriptions painted or scratched onto the plaster walls to preserve them in some way as weather and the elements would eventually destroy them. Most of the mural writings were done in large red or black letters or engraved with a stylus in normal size. Essentially the inscriptions were the early Roman form of advertising: they described events in the amphitheater, rents, offers of rewards for lost items, election propaganda urging citizens to vote for one candidate or another, shop and tavern signs. Often in the shops, the amphitheaters, the homes and in places frequented by a heterogeneous crowd we can find inscriptions that include memos of debts, money received, declarations of love, obscenities, caricatures and dates to remember. This is one of the most interesting aspects of the "dead city" as Pompeii used to be called. The description is wrong because ancient Pompeii is alive and with us today, and will be for posterity through the evidence of the enormous disaster where time suddenly stopped and which is now visible again, in such an unusual way. It is comparable to a real reawakening that perpetuates itself in the interests of the millions of visitors who come away from Pompeii carrying the echoes of a history and a civilization.

THE POMPEIAN HOME AND ITS DECORATIONS

What we have said about the urban structure also applies to the local buildings. Each era left an imprint and we can see them as we proceed with our tour.

Since the Roman element is predominant, we will describe the layout of the *House of the Vettii* that

LAYOUT OF A TYPICAL POMPEIAN HOME
(drawing by Arch. Carpiceci)

TO.: Tabernae and Officinae
1: Atrium
2: Impluvium
3: Compluvium
4: Upper storey
5: Cubiculum
6: Ala
7: Triclinium
8: Andron
9: Viridarium and Peristylium
10: Kitchen
11: Balneum
12: Gynaeceum
13: Triclini, Exedrae and other living rooms
14: Second Peristylium and garden
15: Oecus and Dietae, living rooms

gives a clear and precise idea of the interior arrangement and rooms in most of the luxurious homes and at the same time will acquaint us with the terminology of each sector that we will find in the other homes. The first thing to note is that Roman homes were enclosed by high, windowless walls. They could almost be compared to little fortresses that permitted outsiders to see nothing so that the inhabitants could feel totally at ease.

Here is a list and description of the various rooms: *vestibulum*: this was the area in front of the main door, it protruded from the perimetral wall and was named for the goddess Vesta; *fauces*: the passage that led to the atrium; *atrium*: a rectangular room around which the other rooms of the house were located. We can say that the atrium was the most widely used room in the home: domestic life actually took place here (in other homes the *tablinum*

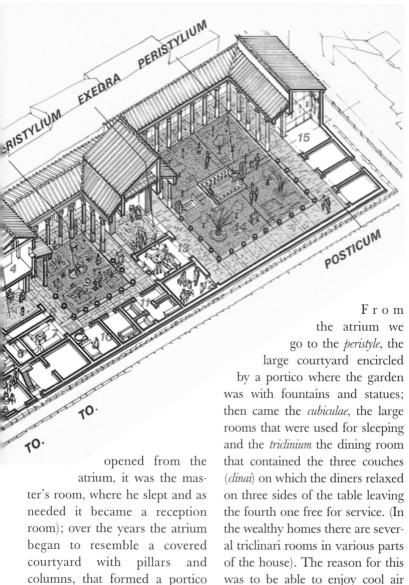

PERISTYLIUM

EXEDRA

PERISTYLIUM

15

POSTICUM

TO.

TO.

TO.

opened from the atrium, it was the master's room, where he slept and as needed it became a reception room); over the years the atrium began to resemble a covered courtyard with pillars and columns, that formed a portico known as the *tetrastyle* if there were four columns (one in each corner) or Corinthian if there were more. Rain came in through the open space, the *compluvium* and it was collected in the *impluvium*, the basin in the middle of the atrium.

From the atrium we go to the *peristyle*, the large courtyard encircled by a portico where the garden was with fountains and statues; then came the *cubiculae*, the large rooms that were used for sleeping and the *triclinium* the dining room that contained the three couches (*clinai*) on which the diners relaxed on three sides of the table leaving the fourth one free for service. (In the wealthy homes there are several triclinari rooms in various parts of the house). The reason for this was to be able to enjoy cool air and sun at any time of year. There were generally two *alae* that opened on the side of the atrium. We do not know what there purpose was. Perhaps in the homes of the wealthy they contained effigies of ancestors. And finally there were the *oecus* the most intimate rooms in the house. Both in the public and private buildings we can see several architectural orders: the Doric, Ionic, Corinthian and Tuscan. The *Doric* order is distinguished by a fluted column that gradually tapers towards the top, with a squared capital; the *Ionic* order has a column supported on a base and fluting separated by cintures and a capital with two circular volutes or scrolls; the *Corinthian* order has a capital decorated with acanthus leaves beneath the Ionic scrolls; the *Tuscan* order was used for rustic buildings, the columns are not fluted and the base is massive. There are also examples of the *composite* order, derived from a fusion of the Ionic and Corinthian styles. Not all the Roman homes were like this. Often there was a shop or tavern in front, according to the owner's occupation. However, in Pompeii there are other examples of primitive, austere dwellings that were gradually modified by Greek and Roman influences. Wealthy houses and villas were enriched with artistic works: paintings, mosaics, small bronze and marble sculptures. These items tell us how advanced were the works not only of the artists proper, but also of the artisans whose skill and inventiveness are revealed in even the most common everyday objects, in bronze bowls and in the finest silverware. It is important to remember the paintings, because whenever Roman painting is mentioned, the reference is almost exclusively to the murals in Pompeii and Herculaneum. Some of the most outstanding are the frescoes in the Villa of the Mysteries, others are now conserved in the Museo Archeologico of Naples: they give a precise idea of each artist in spite of the fact that their names are unknown. This particular type of wall painting can be divided into four styles. The *first style* is known as "incrustation" because it divides the plastered surface of the walls into colored rectangles, imitating marble inlays. This style, which is reminiscent of a Hellenistic fashion died out around the middle of the I century B.C. The *second style* is characterized by "perspective architecture". Various architectural elements such as columns, cornices, and architraves were painted on the wall and appeared to stand out. The areas enclosed by these elements were decorated with landscapes and figured scenes. This style was in fashion from the first half of the I century B.C. until the end of the I century A.D.. The third style is known as the "real wall", here there is no perspective and walls assume the function of ornamental rugs or tapestries. The *third style* developed during the reign of Augustus and seems to have been influenced by Egyptian art after Egypt became a Roman province in 30 B.C.. The *fourth style* is known as "architectural illusionism", it is almost a return to the second, but differs from it because the architectural

Museo Archeologico, Naples - Sleeping Hercules.

elements are rendered with an incredible subtlety creating complex and fantastic scenes rich in lively colors. The fourth style was fashionable from the second half of the I century A.D. on and is the predominant one in Pompeii. Pompeian wall paintings were done in fresco, tempera and encaustic. Frescoes are painted directly onto fresh plaster using ground pigments diluted in water. Tempera involves diluting the pigments in gluey, rubbery substances with egg yolk and wax. The encaustic technique blends

Museo Archeologico di Napoli - Mosaic with sea animals.

the pigments with wax. The painting is then heated so that the wax penetrates and fixes the colors. Artists of the period painted their scenes on a solid-color background that was usually red or yellow, but sometimes even black, green or blue. Roman painting, however, was not limited to large compositions. It extended to decorating the rooms of homes, villas and palaces with familiar scenes, imaginary scenes, still-lifes, lovers and literary subjects and even lively portraits. Roman portraiture already freed itself from Hellenistic influences. It often focused on an entirely personal view that developed in the many scenes of everyday life, big and little, that can be seen throughout Pompeii. Another major decorative art was mosaics, omnipresent in wealthy and even poor homes, albeit in more modest forms.

Pompeii has a vast number of mosaics, on floors as well as walls. And there are different styles: the "opus Alexandrinum", with white and black figures on a solid color background. "Opus tessellatum" describes the style in which tiny tiles were placed in straight lines along the sides; "opus vermiculatum" tiles were arranged in curved lines; "opus signinum" mixed colored stones without any specific pattern; "opus sectile" used tiles cut to size to form the patterns. Pompeian mosaics present a vast range of geometric forms as well as figured emblems inspired by the plant and animal world, hunting and battle scenes, sports and many more.

VESUVIUS: MISFORTUNE AND FORTUNE

Vesuvius was the cause of Pompeii's tragedy and also its fortune. Tragic because of the eruptions which caused the apocalyptic destruction of entire cities like Pompeii, Herculaneum and Stabia, yet fortunate for us because she has preserved her victims almost intact, a silent yet eloquent testimony of a not inglorious past, of an industrious way of life, of a civilization in its most intimate essence. In the Forum, looking towards the Temple of Jupiter, you see it before you, immense, grey, with its two peaks

Above and opposite page: *looking down in the crater of Mt. Vesuvius.*

(Somma and Vesuvius) about 1270 metres high. After the last eruption in 1944 Vesuvius seems to be dormant, and the famous "piume", so beloved of the Neapolitans, has disappeared. Let us hope this sleep lasts thousands of years. The very barrenness, caused by the rivers of lava and ashes evokes respect mixed with fear. But Vesuvius was not always like this. In fact before the terrible eruption of 79 A.D. the summit was covered with woods, where wild boar preyed on game of all species, while the slopes down to the plain were covered with luxuriant vineyards. The delicious Vesuvian wine, of which Pompeians were very proud, was kept in flasks with the inscription «Vesuvinum» to

distinguish it from wines from any other source. Ancient scholars of ancient times like Diodorus Siculus, Strabo and Vitruvius were aware of the volcanic nature of Vesuvius. Seneca and Pliny the Elder could have studied it scientifically, but the former died in 65 A.d., and the latter perished in the famous eruption. There were further eruptions in 202, 472, 512, 635, 993, 1036 and 1139, after which the volcano was silent, and the whole surface was covered once again with forests and farmland until December 1631 when it re-awakened so violently that all crops and houses were destroyed, and there were thousands of human victims. From then on numerous other eruptions fol-

lowed, damaging altering the mountain itself. Then, after 1906, when the lava flow stopped a few feet meters from Torre Annunziata, there were other minor eruptions until the alarming one in 1944.

1-PORTA MARINA AND ANTIQUARIUM

The entrance to the excavations is normally via the Porta Marina, so called because it faces the sea, which has two «fornices» (a fornice is the space defined by an arch). One was meant for pedestrians, as it was less steep, the other for animals. The niche on the right contained the statue of Minerva, the goddess who protected the gates. A few steps on, to the right, is the entrance to the Antiquarium, or Museum, but we suggest that you do not linger here, as we shall return later, but should go on to the actual entrance hall of the Museum, in order to trace the historic development of the city. Everything we shall see has been found during excavations and exemplifies down to the smallest detail the civic and everyday life of the ancient inhabitants. Since we are at the entrance we are looking straight over the terrace, with a beautiful panoramic view of the roads and the mountains of Castellamare. Down the stairs, on the right in a recess between the

building and Porta Marina, is the «Lararium of the Pompeians». Here are busts of the three famous archeologists who concentrated all their study and scientific investigations on Pompeii: Giuseppe Fiorelli, Michele Ruggiero and the German Augustus Mau. In recesses on the northern wall various inscriptions record the history of the principal Pompeian discoveries from 1748 to 1948, and also give the names of those who directed the excavations. On the far wall, carved on slabs of travertine, is the large topographic map of Pompeii (scale: 1:400) commemorating the bicentennial of 13 June 1948; on that occasion the *Antiquarium*, which had been rebuilt, was opened. The building, which goes back to 1861, was destroyed in 1943 by bombings, along with other buildings that had already been excavated. Restoration was carried out under the supervision of Professor Maiuri and his skilled workmen. From the Museum terrace we can see a stretch of the encircling walls dating from the Samnite period (4th century B.C.) which can be recognized by the characteristic technique of using parallelepiped blocks. On the flat space above and below the walls during the era of Augustus and Tiberius stood the magnificent «extramural» Villa of Porta Marina, but it was destroyed in the earthquake of 62 B. C. Today only a small section of the portico, dining and living-rooms remain. If you have time, go down and look

Porta Marina, the entrance to the excavated city.

at what remains of its wall decorations, proof of the greatness and beauty of this aristocratic dwelling Now we return to the Museum and begin our visit. It should be mentioned that not everything that has come to light at Pompeii is in the Antiquarium; many works such as frescoes, mosaics, etc. have been preserved on the site of the digs, while others are kept in the Museo Archeologico in Naples. This applies particularly to the statues, portraits, bronze and various items, that are of inestimable value to scholars and those interested in the study of ancient Rome. Because of the brevity of this guide it, should be noted that we will point out only the most important sights, so that when the visit is over you will have seen the best of ancient Pompeii.

ENTRANCE

On the walls are decorative sculptures, amongst which should

Antiquarium - Pediment and altar from the Sanctuary of Dionysius.

be noted the *Satyr with a Club* and *Eros with a Shell*. On the walls there are also mural maps showing the chronological development of the excavations from 1748 to 1948.

FIRST ROOM

Devoted to the Pompeii of the pre-Samnite period, it displays all that has been discovered from the early period of both the city and the countryside around the valley of the Sarno. The furniture is displayed in showcases: in cases 1-6, the funeral trappings of the Iron Age, The Etrusco-Campanian «buccheri» and bronze ornaments. In cases 2-5 there are fine architectural terracottas which date from the oldest period of the city, fragments of sculpture and painted glass from the facing of the Doric temple of the Triangular Forum and the Temple of Apollo, friezes and fragments of black and red figured Greek vases. All these give evidence of the customs, habits and religions, as well as of the existence of major monuments of the times.

SECOND ROOM

This display illustrates Samnite Pompeii during the certain political independence of the first period, while in the second, the Greek influence in art, culture and religion is evident. On the walls are

Antiquarium - Plaster cast of a young victim of the eruption.

lovely capitals and, in the space in the passage, the *Sphinx* by an Italo-Campanian sculptor. On one side is the beautiful capital, girded with ivy, with the figure of a *Maenad* (the Maenads were female followers of Dionysius) and on the other *Winged Eros*. On the opposite side is another capital with a bust of *Maenad with Timpanum* and *Satyr with Reedpipe*. On the left-hand wall we can admire the pediment and the altar of the Sanctuary of Dionysius found near the Pompeii railway station in 1947.

ROOM OF LIVIA

In the centre is the statue of Livia, a cult statue which was found in the Villa of the Mysteries. In the corners are *portraits of Cornelius Rufus* and *Vesonius Primus* and *Silenus holding the Young Bacchus in his arms*. Opposite is a *portrait of Marcellus*, nephew of Augustus.

THIRD ROOM

Dedicated to Roman Pompeii, this room contains domestic furniture. In the center are two basins, the brass one was found in the House of Menander and in the corners are bronze statuettes of cupids from the House of the Vettii. In showcase 8, various types of bronzeware and a series of bone hair clasps are displayed. Outside, are lovely *situlas* (vessels

Antiquarium - Cast of a dog.

for carrying liquids) with small palms and griffins found in the House of Menander. In case 9, ornaments in gold, bone and carved ivory; 10, statuettes of divinities; 11, a statue of Pan and furniture found in the House of Paquius Proculus and P. Cornelius Tegete, and in 12 is an extremely interesting gold and silver toilet set. In the passageway are several striking casts of humans positioned as they tried to protect themselves from the noxious fumes. There are a beautiful semi-nude body of a young woman, supine, with her head resting on her arm and a watch-dog, chained up outside the House of Vesonius Primus, desperately attempting to escape.

FOURTH ROOM

This also is devoted to Roman Pompeii, but this collection illustrates interesting aspects of the commercial life of the city. Look at case 13 with tools belonging to a bronze and silver-smith; case 14 contains maritime equipment found when the beach of Pompeii was explored; case 15, supplies for factories and shops; case 16, remains of food (the dough ready

Antiquarium - Casts of wheel and a tree.

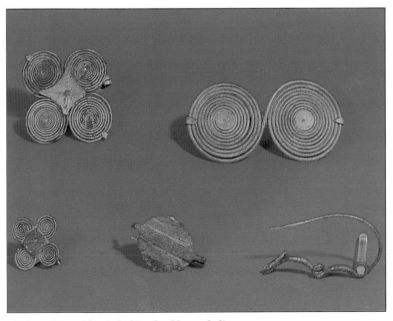

Antiquarium - Metal clothing buckles and clips.

Antiquarium - Cast of a mule-driver.

for the oven of Modestus is charred, but the shape of the loaves is still visible); case 17, various mechanical devices such as locks, hinges, taps, clasps, scales, and an example of a heating appliance; in case 18, a series of surgical instruments and coins and silverware, found in the big gymnasium, belonging to the people flee-ing. In the center is a model of a country house with the equipment for a wine business. It is now time for you to return to the Porta Marina entrance where there are more clay casts: notice the cupboard, the wheel, the tree, and the mule-driver wrapped in his rough cloak in an effort to save himself from the shower of fire and ashes.

The Basilica.

2-TEMPLE OF VENUS

As soon as you come out of the Antiquarium, on your way to the excavated area, you will note a Pompeian olive-oil press on your left, and further on, stop at the first gate on the right, from which you can see the site of the temple dedicated to Venus, protectress of the city. Ruined by the earthquake, it had not yet been restored at the time of the famous eruption and little remains of the original building.

3-BASILICA

The most important public building in Pompeii, the Basilica was used for the administration of justice and for the meetings of businessmen who gathered here to discuss their affairs. The building is rectangular, measuring 24 by 55 meters, with 28 huge brick columns dividing it into three naves. At the far end is the podium of the Tribunal with two rows of columns, proof of Greek influence. It has been extremely difficult for historians to establish

The Basilica and the double-order colonnade encircling the Forum.

the dating of this building, but the recovery of various tablets bearing the Oscan seal, and tests made on the foundations have led to the conclusion that it was probably constructed about the year 120 B.C., that is in the pre-Roman period.

4-TEMPLE OF APOLLO

On the western side of the Forum is the Temple of Apollo, but before entering we shall walk further along the arcade itself, where almost at the end of the temple, in a niche in the outside wall, we can find the *mensa ponder-*

aria, a table with hollows to standardize weights and measures. A little further on, a row of pillars in brick marks the site of building which probably served as a storehouse for grains; and at the end in the corner to the left, a large latrine. A bit farther are two underground rooms which it seems, were used for the municipal treasury. Turning back, we now enter the Temple of Apollo, which already existed in the Samnite epoch, and was later dedicated to Apollo (6th century). During the Imperial period substantial modifications were made according to the architectural and decorative concepts of the time. As we can see, it had a portico of 48 columns, and in front of the stairs

Temple of Apollo - Apollo the Archer, copy of the original which is in the Museo Archeologico, Naples.

is the *ara*, the altar, which in Greek and Roman temples was always in an open space in front of the temple; to the left of the stairs, on top of an Ionic column is a sun-dial constructed at the expense of the «diumviri» L. Sepunius and M. Erennius. At the top of the stairs there is a Corinthian colonnade of six columns along the front, and the entrance to the «*cella*», the innermost part of the temple where the images of the divinity were kept. As we turn back before descending the stairs, observe the arcade in front, and the bronze

The Temple of Apollo.

statues of *Apollo* to the left, *Diana* to the right. These are copies; the originals are housed in the Museo Archeologico in Naples.

5-THE FORUM

This was the heart of the political, religious and social life of Pompeii, around which were constructed the various public buildings we are going to see. The rectangular square is 38 meters wide and 142 meters long; and at the time of its destruction it was probably sur-

rounded on three sides by a big arcade, on top of which was an open gallery supported by smaller columns. On the fourth side was the Temple of Jupiter. To the south there is a section of trabeation (this is the part overlying the columns and consists of architrave, frieze and cornice) from the Samnite era, while the columns and trabeations of the eastern and western sides date from the Roman period. On the southern side of the arcade are several pedestals on which, at one time there were the statues of important citizens; on the western side there was a much larger pedestal which was the tribune of the orators. It takes little to imagine

Aerial view of the Forum; below: *another view of the Forum with Mt. Vesuvius in the background.*

The Municipal Offices.

how magnificent this square must have been, with the great arcade covered with precious marbles, dotted with statues, and the whole area paved in travertine, and surrounded by splendid public buildings. Above all we think of it as the lively center of public life - a meeting point for city dwellers of every class, and farmers from the countryside under Pompeian administration.

6-MUNICIPAL OFFICES

Beside the Basilica are the three rooms where the Municipal Offices were situated, and where the «*duumviri*», the aediles and the Municipal Council were based. The central room probably served as the public archives, and in the larger room the council meetings were held. All these areas must have been originally covered with marble facing.

7-COMITIUM

On the corner of Via dell'Abbondanza is the Comitium, where the elections for public offices were held. Proceeding on, turning right into the Vicolo dei Dodici Dei, we find the **House of the Wild Boar**, so called because on the floor is a mosaic of a wild boar being attacked by two dogs. The house has interesting decorations in marble and mosaic, beautiful examples of which are in the hall, and busts on medallions in the tablinum.

The portico in front of the Building of Eumachia.

Behind is a large portico with a garden, on the southern side of which is a spacious exedra for meetings.

8-BUILDING OF EUMACHIA

On returning to the Comitium we find the Building of Eumachia, which takes its name from the inscription over the door facing Via dell'Abbondanza, saying that the cost of construction of the building was borne by the priestess Eumachia. It was the seat of the *guild of the Fullones,* the guild of cloth-makers, launderers and dyers. Eumachia dedicated it to Concordia Augusta and to «Pietà» (both personifications of Livia, wife of Augustus). Due to its large membership, the guild had an overwhelming influence on the city's commercial and political activities.

We enter from the Forum side: the façade has two rows of columns and a fine marble doorway, adorned with spiral acanthus motifs, which leads into a spacious courtyard. Originally a statue of the empress stood in the middle of the three apses at the far end. Beyond the porch was the *cryptoporticus,* a closed arcade used as a promenade, and as a link to other buildings. Here the beautiful *statue of Eumachia* which the Fullones commissioned in her honor was excavated. The statue is now in the Museo Archeologico in Naples.

The Temple of Vespasian; below: *the marble ara or altar, with a relief carving of the sacrifice of a bull.*

9-TEMPLE OF VESPASIAN

This was dedicated to the worship of the imperial cult. Note the beautiful *ara* in marble, with a relief representing a sacrifice. One can see the sacrificing priest, the *victimarius* (who leads the victim to the altar), the lictors, a flute-player, and young ceremonial ministers. In a shrine at the back is a statue dedicated to the cult.

10-SANCTUARY OF THE LARES

After the famous earthquake of 62 B.C. this

The Macellum and the beautiful marble-columned portico.

sanctuary was built in atonement and dedicated to the gods who protected the city (*Lares publici*).

11-MACELLUM

This was a covered market used for the sale of foodstuffs, especially meat and fish, and its construction dates back to the imperial era. In front, looking out on the Forum, is an elegant porch of marble columns where the money-changers carried on their business. Inside is another porch that collapsed during the earthquake of 62, in the center of which is a circular construction with a water-basin, while beyond there were places dedicated to imperial worship. On the right is the section reserved for the sale of fish. Also, the Macellum was decorated with frescoes of mythological scenes, and around the walls was a frieze showing various kinds of foods. *Statues of Octavia*, sister of Augustus, and her son, *Marcellus* were found in one of the rooms here; they are now in the Museo Archeologico in Naples.

12-TEMPLE OF JUPITER

Dedicated to three divinities, Jupiter, Juno and Minerva, this temple dates from the 2nd century B.C., and was the Capitol Building of Pompeii. It must have been a beautiful and imposing structure, fronted by a double flight of steps and a pronaos (atrium surrounded by columns) crowned by Corinthian columns. Inside was a large cella in which was found an enormous *marble head of Jupiter*, now in the Museo Archeologico in Naples. Half destroyed by the earthquake, it was being restored at the time of the catastrophic Vesuvian eruption. At the side are two honorary arches dedicated to the imperial family, perhaps to Tiberius and Germanicus.

13-FORUM BATHS

Passing through the arch to the right of Jupiter's Temple, we find the snack bar. Opposite are the archeologists' offices where scholars may apply for fur-

ther information. Straight ahead, to the left, at No. 12 Via delle Terme, is the entrance to the Forum Baths. They are not especially large, but give us an example of how an important public service was organized, especially since they are in excellent state of preservation. The baths are divided into two sections: one for men and one for women. A small corridor leads into the men's changing-room; note the niches for clothes and the seats where the people could wait their turn. From here they entered the «*frigidarium*» decorated in stucco (where they had cold baths in a tub). Returning to the changing-room, on the left is the entrance to the «*tepidarium*» (the room between the hot and cold baths) with a stucco barrel

The Temple of Jupiter flanked by triumphal arches.

Forum Baths - the "tepidarium".

Forum Baths - the "calidarium".

The Temple of Fortuna Augusta.

vault, and niches in the walls adorned with terracotta «*telamones*» (human figures used in architecture to support trabeations and cornices). Note the *bronze brazier* used to heat this area, which was constructed at the expense of Marcus Nigidius Vaccula. From the tepidarium they would enter the «*calidarium*» (for hot or Turkish baths), with a double wall for the passage of hot air, and a large tub, on the side of which are bronze inscriptions with the names of the donors who had it placed here in 3-4 A.D.: «Cnaeus Melissaeus Aper and M. Staius Rufus» (the tub cost 5240 sestertii). Also one should not overlook the stuccoes on the ceiling. These baths, which also boasted a gym-nasium, were constructed in the initial period of Roman colonization, in 80 B.C.

14-TEMPLE OF FORTUNA AUGUSTA

 It was dedicated to the imperial cult, and was constructed in the year 3 B.C. by Marcus Tullius, a military tribune elected on numerous occasions to public office, and thus an important figure in the city. You reach the temple by climbing a staircase with an *ara*, coming to the pronaos with six Corinthian columns, and in the rear of a small inner area, there is the cella which

The House of the Faun - Atrium.

contains the shrine with the inscription of the donor. In the niches on the side walls were four statues.

15-HOUSE OF THE FAUN

Turning right from the Temple of the Goddess Fortuna, into the street of the same name, is (at Nos. 2-5) the House of the Faun. In the impluvium a beautiful small bronze representing a *dancing faun* was discovered: hence the house's name. The bronze we now see is a copy; the original is in the Museo Archeologico in Naples. This is one of the largest and most sumptuous dwellings of the Samnite era (2nd century B.C.), but all the architectural elements betray Greek and Italic influence. Precious mosaics have been removed from this house for preservation in the Naples Museum, including the famous *Battle of Alexander*. Entering, the *Latin Salve* (welcome) greets your eye. The hall floor is coloured marble, and on the walls is a mock marble facing. High up are two *Lararia* executed in stucco. Next is the grandiose atrium with fine wall decorations and off this are the alee paved with mosaic. Adjoining the tablinum are the dining-rooms, then come the small tetrastyle atrium, and the first peristyle composed of twenty-eight Ionic columns, in the center of

The House of the Faun - exedra and peristyles; below: **Museo Archeologico, Naples - Battle of Alexander from the floor of the exedra in the House of the Faun.**

Opposite page: **Museo Archeologico, Naples - Dancing Faun, from the House of the Faun.**

sun-dial and sacellum of the Lararium. No. 48 is the **House of the Hunt**, an interesting dwelling of the pre-Roman period, which has, inside the entrance, reconstructions in the fourth style. In the atrium are the seasons *Winter* and *Autumn* and lovely paintings of mythological subjects in the cubiculum and the right wing, while at the end of the garden is the huge fresco which gave the house its name: a beautiful country scene of a hunt.

16-HOUSE OF THE TRAGIC POET

If you have time, before visiting the House of the Tragic Poet, pass under the *Arch of Caligula* on Via del Mercurio, along which, only a short way down on the right and side at No. 7 is the **House of the Anchor,** named for the mosaic of an anchor at the entrance. Above all you should visit the lovely garden in the longer part of which are apsed niches, while the upper part is enclosed within a graceful colonnade. No. 1 is the **Tavern** or **Caupona**, with a typical example of a Pompeian shop counter, and a storeroom for the kitchenware and cooking tools. Inside is the meeting-place for clients, decorated with paintings in the popular style portraying various aspects of tavern life - note the *Four Drinkers sit-*

which is a fountain. In back is the exedra (the floor had the famous «Battle of Alexander» mosaic). From here and the exedra you enter other triclinia. To the right of the peristyle are the servants'quarters (kitchen, bath and a stable) and along a corridor there is another large peristyle with a garden. Leaving the House of the Faun, on Via della Fortuna, we find at No. 59 the **House of the Black Wall** named after the room behind the peristyle which contains charming panels of *cupids* against a black background. At No. 57 is the **House of the Figured Capitals** a beautiful house of the Samnite period. The pillars at the entrance have fine capitals with Bacchic figures, and beyond, in the garden, there is a

Preceding page, from the top: *House of the Tragic Poet - the atrium, tablinum and garden* and *the House of the Great Fountain - the fountain with mosaics.* Above: *House of the Little Fountain - the fountain with mosaic.*

ting at the Dinner Table. No. 22 the **House of the Great Fountain** decorated with fine mosaics, fountain with a mosaic niche and a *statuette of a young boy with a dolphin* (a copy, the original is in the Museo Archeologico). At No. 23 is the **House of the Little Fountain** with a graceful nymphaeum (temple of nymphs, and in this case a fountain consecrated to nymphs). On the walls there is a lovely fresco of a landscape, noteworthy for its fine polychromes. At Nos. 20-21 is a spacious Fullonica, for washing and dyeing. Going back through the Arch of Caligula, we find, to the right, the **House of the Tragic Poet.** In the tablinum a mosaic representing a teacher of

House of Pansa - the peristyle; below: **Ovens and mills on the Via Consolare.**

lyric or tragic theater was discovered, and this gave the house its name. The house is famous for the frescoes of heroic and mythological subjects (amongst which the *Sacrifice of Iphigenia*), which were found on the walls of the atrium

and peristyle, and have been placed in the Naples Museum. The house is familiar to the general public because the writer Bulwer Lytton used it for Glaucus' house in «The Last Days of Pompeii». The house belonged to a middle class Pompeian who became wealthy through his activities as a merchant. Notice the mosaic depicting a watch dog with the inscription *cave canem* (beware of the dog), and in the atrium the marble basin of the impluvium, around it are the various cubiculae and the staircases which go up to the second floor. Beyond the tablinum is a small porch and garden with a Lararium. To the right of the porch, after the kitchen, is the dining room of the triclinium,

House of Sallust - atrium.

the walls of which are decorated with the following mythological subjects: *Venus contemplating a nest of Cupids, Mars and Olympus, Theseus Abandoning Ariadne* and *Dido and Aeneas*.

17-HOUSE OF PANSA

This imposing house of the Samnite period once belonged to Cnaeus Alleius Nigidius Maius, but it was later converted into an apartment building by its last owner (whose name has come down to us from a «to let» sign). All along Vicolo della Fullonica and Vicolo di Modesto there are numerous shops and places for rent. Nothing has remained of the original decoration. Through the entrance is the atrium and the usual impluvium, the tablinum and the peristyle with a large pool in the middle, and further on, a spacious living room. Beyond is the orchard, today used for a plant nursery.

18-HOUSE OF SALLUST

From the House of Pansa take the Via Consolare. At No. 3 is the House of the Baker, with equipment for making bread.

At No. 4, is the **House of Sallust** from the Samnite period, which belonged to A. Cossius Libanius. Here too there are shops on either side of the entrance, while inside is a large atrium in the Tuscan style with an impluvium in the tablinum and in one of the cubiculae are remains of wall-painting of the first style. Very different is the decoration of the small peristyle with hexagonal columns on the southern side. In the gynaeceum, the place reserved for women, one of the walls was frescoed with the *Myth of Actaeon surprising Diana at her bath*, but it was destroyed in World War II.

19-HOUSE OF THE SURGEON

Further along on Via Consolare at No. 13 is a building called «*Statio Saliniensium*», where there presumably was a salt warehouse, and the guild for those connected with the salt-works located on the coast. At No. 10 is

the façade of the **House of the Surgeon**, so called because surgical instruments (of inestimable value for the study of ancient surgical equipment) were discovered here. The collection is in the Museo Archeologico. The house is an excellent example of the use of limestone dating back to the 4th and 3rd centuries B.C. Shortly after is the **House of the Vestals**, which is interesting for its elegant entrance-hall; then we come to the **Porta Ercolano**, and then to the Via dei Sepolcri, which we shall return to when describing the suburban Villas. The Porta Ercolano, which was first called *Porta Saliniensis*, consists of three arches, the middle one for carriages and the two side ones for pedestrians. It was certainly constructed over an earlier one in the time of the Romans.

20-HOUSE OF MELEAGER

From Porta Ercolano follow the inside of the solid city wall, and take the fourth street which is *Via di Mercurio*. At No. 24 is the **House of Apollo**, the façade of which is true to the Italic type but which has decorations from a later Pompeian period. Behind the tablinum note the lovely fountain, and in the garden a cubiculum with a mosaic of *The Recognition of Achilles at Scyros* and a landscape. Inside are paintings of the fourth style, with scenes showing the *Musical Contest between Apollo and Mars*. Opposite, at No. 2, is the **House of Meleager**, a beautiful aristocratic dwelling of the Samnite period with inside decoration typical of the fourth style. Do not overlook the beautiful peristyle, in the center of which is a large garden pool with statuettes. To the right of the peristyle there are

Via di Mercurio.

House of Meleager - the peristyle.

three large rooms; the central one has a Greek style arcade, and probably served as a luxurious reception-room. Beyond this is an imposing triclinium with rich, but unfortunately very much deteriorated decoration. Next door, Nos. 3-5 is the **House of the Centaur,** composed of three buildings; the cubiculum to the right is interesting, as it has wall decorations in the first style. Opposite, at No. 18, the **House of Adonis**, is worth a visit for the beautiful painting on the garden wall depicting *Venus with the Wounded Adonis*, while in a room on the south side are frescoes in the third and fourth styles among which is a painting of *The Toilet of Hermaphrodite*. Going along Via di Mercurio to Nos. 6-7, we enter the **House of Castor and Pollux**. Here note the magnificent atrium with twelve Corinthian columns, and, beyond the tablinum, the porch with a shrine. To the right of the tablinum there is a room decorated with paintings of

House of Castor and Pollux - the atrium.

The Birth of Adonis, Scilla and Minos; to the left are *Apollo and Daphne,* and *Silenus with Nymph and the Young Bacchus.* On the right side of the atrium is a peristyle with a basin in the middle, and on the walls pictorial decorations of the fourth style. A short way along Via di Mercurio, turn right into Vicolo di Mercurio, where at No. 10 is the **House of the Labyrinth**, an aristocratic house from Samnite times. The name derives from the *scene of Theseus and the Minotaur* depicted in a mosaic on the floor of a room off the great peristyle. The house has two halls, the principal one in tetrastyle, the other in Tuscan style. Beyond the large peristyle are the reception rooms, the middle ones with a Corinthian colonnade, as well as the room containing the mosaic with the myth of Theseus. The west side was converted for commercial use, as can be seen from the oven equipment and a mill, while in back is a private bath.

21-HOUSE OF THE VETTII

To get the most from your visit, follow the numbers on the plan we have included here below. This building, once a luxurious aristocratic dwelling, belonged to two merchants, probably brothers, whose business was very prosperous: Aulus Vettius Restitutus and Aulus Vettius Conviva. In building their splendid house, however, they did everything they could to deny their origin as merchants; they felt they were gentle-men and wished to be considered as such. The house provides the visitor with a truly complete picture of the Pompeian-Roman house of the wealthy classes, especially when we consider it was almost entirely restored after the disastrous earthquake of 62 A.D. The House of the Vetti is famous world over for its unique wall decorations in the fourth style. Skillful excavation has permitted the reconstruction of the whole building and, by means of restoration and re-touching, the genuine atmosphere of a real home has been recreated. We enter the hall

HOUSE OF THE VETTII

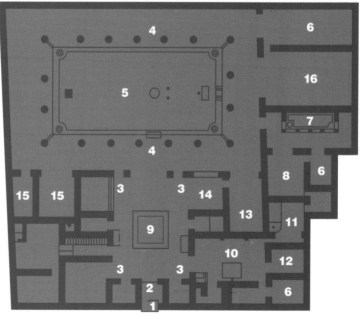

1 - Vestibule	6 - Cubiculum	11 - 12 - Kitchen
2 - Fauces	7 - Peristyle	13 - Triclinium
3 - Atrium	8 - Triclinium	14 - Alae
4 - Peristyle	9 - Impluvium	15 - Oecus
5 - Garden	10 - Lararium	16 - 17 - Triclinium

House of the Vetti - Priapus, god of fertility, frescoed in the vestibule.

House of the Vetti - Mourning Ciparissus.

where we note a painting of *Priapus*, god of fertility. The superstitious Vetti had it painted to protect them from the evil-eye of those envious of their prosperity. Then, through the *fauces*, we enter the hall with an impluvium in the centre to collect the water falling from the roof; on the sides are two strong boxes where money and silverware were kept, and on the pillars and plinths are lovely figures of cupids and maidens. In the small room to the left of the entrance is a frieze of a fish pond and underneath it, two small paintings: *Ariadne Deserted* and *Eros and Leander*. In the room next door there are others: *Mourning Ciparissus*, *Pan* and *Love fighting*, *Jupiter Enthroned* and *Leda and Danae*. We continue to the two wings of the atrium: the one on the

House of the Vetti - Lararium.

left has panels with *Cockfighting*, while the right-hand one shows medals, small yet expressive, with the heads of *Medusa* and *Silenus*. To the right of the atrium is a small hall with a temple *Lararium* decorated in stucco, and there is a painting of a *Genius*, the head of the family, between two *Lares*, and underneath a *snake* approaching the altar laden with funeral offerings. Then come the cook's quarters and in a small courtyard, is the kitchen, the hearth contains a bronze trivet and a cauldron. Opposite the kitchen is another small room with erotic paintings. From here we move to the women's quarters with a triclinium and an elegant little portico. Now we come outside into a large peristyle which encloses a beautiful garden with flower-beds,

House of the Vetti - Peristyle and garden.

statuettes in bronze and marble, and fountains. The interesting thing about this garden is that the waterways were not designed as such; during excavations it was found that old water pipes underneath faithfully followed the lay-out of the garden. The Vetti were able to see the peristyle and the garden in all its colourful beauty from the large triclinium where symposia used to be held. On entering this room we must admire the wall decoration, which is on a red base, set off by pilasters with black bands. Each square probably had a paintingi n the center, on the theme of dining, but nothing has remained of this decoration. On the longer part, on a cornice above the plinth, is a delightful series of *cupids* doing various tasks. From

House of the Vetti - Two details of the frieze with scenes of Cupids, in the large triclinium.

House of the Vetti - Detail of a wall painting, red squares and black pillars, in the large triclinium.

Opposite page from the top: **House of the Vettii - Painting in the "oecus"** and **"Daedalus showing Pasiphae the Wooden Cow".**

right to left: cupids aiming stones at a target, entwining and buying flowers, absorbed in preparing and selling perfumed oils; the chariot race; cupid metalworkers and goldsmiths, following the trade of fullones, some celebrating the Vestals; gathering grapes; the triumph of Bacchus, and cupids selling wine. Beneath the cupid frieze are panels with *Pyches.* In the central squares of the long walls are panels with mythological subjects: on the right-hand wall *Agamemnon about to kill the Sacred Hind* and *Apollo slaying the Python,* while on the left are *Orestes*

House of the Vetti - The Infant Hercules strangling the snakes.

and Pylades before Thoas and Iphigenia. On the side walls mythological romantic couples: *Perseus and Andromeda, Dionysius and Ariadne, Apollo and Daphne, Poseidon and Amymone.* Leaving the large triclinium we go into the smaller one with lovely wall paintings: on the left *Dedalus showing Pasiphae the Wooden Cow,* opposite *Ixion tied by Zeus to the wheel in the presence of Juno,* to the right *Epiphany of Dionysius and Ariadne.* On the other side of the atrium, in the largest roorn, on the left is *The Infant Hercules strangling the*

Snakes and opposite *Pentheus being torn to pieces by the Bacchants* and on the right *The Torture of Dirce.*

22-HOUSE OF THE GOLDEN CUPIDS

This was the aristocratic dwelling of Cnaeus Poppeus Abitus, and it name derives from the decoration in the cubiculum, the walls of which depict *cupids* en-

House of the Golden Cupids - Garden.

graved on gold plates. Here we find ourselves in what was the house of a noble family of the Neronian period. Through the entrance, the floor of the right hand cubiculum is decorated with *Leda with the Swan* and *Narcissus at the Fountain,* while to the left is *Mercury in Flight.* On the back wall of the tablinum is a representation of *Paris and Helen at Sparta.* From the hall we pass into the elegant peristyle. The west side is raised owing to the unevenness of the terrain, and this creates a beautiful effect. Between the columns hang the so-called «*oscilla*», or marble discs with various designs. In the south wing is a finely carved marble fragment with *Silenus* and others. Between the atrium and the peristyle is the triclinium, the walls of which have pictures of the third style: left, *Thetis in Vulcan's Workshop,* on the back wall, *Jason, wearing only one sandal, before Pelias,* right *Achilles, Briseis and Patroclus in the tent.* In the center of the west porch is a large triclinium, with a small room on either side. In the righthand one

House of the Golden Cupids - Venus Fishing.

House of the Golden Cupids - Peristyle portico.

are mural paintings *Diana and Actaeon, Leda, Venus Fishing*. In the north porch, near a room decorated in black, is a cubiculum with *cupids*. The **House of the Cupids** faces onto Via del Vesuvio, whose paving-stones are deeply scored by the continuous passing of carriages. At the end, on the left, is **Porta Vesuvio**, one of the most important city gates. It was damaged in the earthquake, and at the time of the great eruption was being restored. Next to it is the building housing the storage tank for water supplied

from a branch of the aqueduct from the Serino River.

23-HOUSE OF ORPHEUS

Returning from the Porta Vesuviana along Via Stabiana, after the House of the Cupids, No. 28 is the *Gambling-House*, with an emblem of a vase on the façade between two erotic pictures. This was where the dice-players and the young of both

The intersection of Via Stabiana and Via dell'Abbondanza.

sexes gathered, and the owner must have been able to make a fortune from loans. No. 21 is the *Fullonica*, a laundry and dyeing plant, which was converted into an aristocratic home. No. 20, the **House of Orpheus**, which belon- ged to Vesonius Primus, was built in the Samnite period, but was almost entirely rebuilt in the impe- rial era. Its name comes from the large fresco on the end wall of the peristyle which shows *Orpheus amongst the beasts*.

24-HOUSE OF CAECILIUS JUCUNDUS

Opposite the House of Orpheus, at No. 26, is the **House of Lucius Caecilius Jucundus**, well-known by scholars not only for its beauty but also for the important material discovered providing information about banking. In fact, a box was unearthed in which there were perfectly preserved wax tablets used as receipts and also a beautiful life-like *bronze bust* of the owner of the house, who was an experienced and well-known banker.

House of the Silver Wedding - the "oecus tetrastylus" with the vaulted ceiling.

The portrait on display is a copy; the original is in the archeological museum. A wise administrator, Caecilius Jucundus also wanted to have a beautiful home. The mar-ble reliefs of the Chapel of the Lares, in the hall on the left, are votive offerings: one represents the *Temple of Jupiter* and the *Triumphal Arch of the Forum*, the other *Porta Vesuvio with «tripartitore» of water collapsing after the earthquake*. The herma (pillar bearing the head of a man; the name derives from the fact that the god Hermes was originally represented thus) by the tablinum supported a *bronze bust of the owner* erected by a grateful freedman. Here are some of the finest third style decorations. Leaving the house of the bankers, we come to the Orpheus. Crossing and then on the left, at No. 21, the **House of the Young Bull**. Its beautiful façade dates back to the Samnite period. At the entrance you can see the ingenious method adopted to keep out the glances of prying passers-by: the double door in which a smaller door gave access to the house. On the wall at the back of the peristyle are remains of a nymph (in three niches between pilasters faced with mosaic).

25-HOUSE OF THE SILVER WEDDING

Proceeding along Via di Nola we come to No. 1: the **House of Queen Margherita**, with beautiful pictures in the rooms along the sides of the tablinum. To the left are *Leda and the Swan, Poseidon and Amymone, Jupiter and Danae, Meleager and Atalanta*, to the right *Narcissus, Ariadne deserted* and *The Madness of Lycurgus*.
Taking the small lane to the right

we come to the **House of the Silver Wedding**, named thus because it was excavated in 1893, the year the sovereigns of Italy celebrated their Silver Wedding Anniversary. This beautiful patrician house dates back to the Samnite epoch, but both the structures and decoration were modified in the imperial age. The initial impression is of dignified grandeur, there is an imposing tetrastyle entrance hall, with enormous Corinthian columns, decorated in the second style. Through the atrium is the peristyle, the most luxurious part of which is the south side: there are four columns supporting the ceiling of the impressive room, whose walls are frescoed with architectural motifs of the second style. In the ambulatory there are cubiculae decorated in the same style, and a room with black walls. There is also a private bath, with a calidarium and a tepidarium; and in the garden a tub for cold baths.

26-HOUSE OF LUCRETIUS FRONTO

In this small imperial house there is extensive pictorial decoration skillfully carried out in the third style. In the tablinum, besides the panels on rural themes, there are two small paintings: *The Wedding of Venus and Mars*

House of Lucrezio Frontone - The Wedding of Venus and Mars and (below)
The Triumph of Bacchus.

and *The Triumph of Bacchus*. In the large triclinium is *Neoptolemus killed by Orestes at Delphi* and in a room to the right of the tablinum *Narcissus at the Fountain* and *Pero nurturing her old father Micone*. To the right of the atrium are *Theseus and Ariadne* and *The Toilet of Venus*.

27-HOUSE OF THE GLADIATORS

With the construction of the Amphitheatre, the Pompeians became fanatical about gladiatorial games; and it was for this reason that this house was converted for the gladiators' families' use. The peristyle is decorated with *hunting and mythological scenes* and on the columns are scrawled inscriptions which gladiators made to boast of exploits in the ring and in bed. As we go out, to the left, we see the single arch **Porta di Nola** in the distance (Samnite era). At the top of the arch is a head of Minerva.

28-HOUSE OF OBELIUS FIRMUS

A lovely house from the Samnite period, it has a double hall and a double entrance. In the impluvium is a charming statue of a *Satyr* (a cast, the original is in the archeological museum). To the right are the Lararium and a safe. Behind the peristyle a large room and cubiculum are decorated with paintings of the second style.

29-HOUSE OF THE CENTENNIAL

So called because it was discovered in 1879, the eighteenth centennial of the famous eruption, the building consists of three dwellings. It underwent various transformations in the imperial period before and after the earthquake of 62. Worthy of note are the spacious Tuscan entrance hall, its mosaic floor, and the impluvium. The walls are decorated with fourth style pictures on theatrical subjects. On either side of the tablinum are rooms with artful decoration. From here we enter the peristyle, on the walls of which are yellow panels bearing the emblems of *Juno, Apollo* and *Minerva*. In the garden there is a pool, in which originally a charming little bronze of a *Satyr with Wineskin* (now in the archeological museum) was placed. At the end of the peristyle is a little court with a delighful fountain adorned with hunting scenes, garden views, and a fish pool. On the west side, by way of a narrow hallway, we reach a suite. In the atrium there is a Lararium which originally con-

Preceding page, from the top: ***House of Obelius Firmus - the tetrastyle atrium*** and ***the House of the Centennial - erotic scenes.***
Above: ***House of the Centennial - Fresco.***

tained a painting of *Bacchus at the foot of a wooded and grapevine-covered mountain* (now in the archeological museum) which might well be a depiction of Vesuvius before the eruption. There is also a bath; and

several other rooms. In one there are three small paintings on a background: *Theseus and the Minotaur*, *Hermaphroditus* and *Silenus and Orestes, Pylades and Iphigenia*. There is also a room with erotic drawings.

Via Stabiana.

30-CENTRAL BATHS

We have already spoken about the lay-out of the Forum Baths. Those we are about to enter constitute the most modern version of the Roman baths, since they were constructed after 62 A.D. in accordance with the dictates of the most exacting taste of those times. Unfortunately they were never completed. These baths covered a whole *«insula»*, that is, one of the blocks into which the urban area was divided, and to the north and east there are numerous shops. The main entrance is from Via Stabiana, and opens immediately into a large palestra. On the far side is the *«natatio»*, the swimming pool, and to the south the latrine and changing-rooms. On the eastern side is another large changing-room; the *tepidarium* and the *laconicum* for Turkish baths, are circular, with a dome. Next is the *calidarium*, with apsed rectangular niches and windows to provide light. This is a new feature, and together with the laconicum, shows us the differences in construction and lay-out that came about with respect to earlier versions of the baths.

31-HOUSE OF MARCUS LUCRETIUS

Via Stabiana No. 5 is the **House of Marcus Lucretius**, a Pompeian citizen of some note, who was in fact a *«decurione»* (commander of a decuria in the Roman cavalry) and a priest of Mars. His house was consistent with his dignity of office. In the atrium, on the right, is the Lararium opposite a large tablinum; and behind, the garden. As it slopes upward, you can admire the beautiful fountain, as well as niches and lawns with hermae and attractive statues representing *Silenus with a wineskin, Satyrs, Pan, Cupid riding a dolphin,* and *figures of animals.* The house used to contain beautiful fourth

House of Marcus Lucretius.

syle paintings most of which have been removed and placed in the archeological museum. The paintings on the tablinum are extant: *Triumph of Bacchus followed by a Satyr and Victory.*

32-HOUSE OF GAVIUS RUFUS

From Vicolo del Panettiere we enter the area which was the oldest and the least rep-

utable in Pompeii. The **House of Gavius Rufus** deserves a look although it differs from the others only to a slight degree.

33-BAKERY OF MODESTUS

There is no doubt that the numerous bakeries played an important part in Pompeii's business life. It is also very likely that some of the bread was sent

Preceding page: ***House of the Bear - mosaic fountain.***
Above: ***House of Siricus - fresco of Neptune and Apollo.***

out to the various retailers and to nearby towns. The Bakery, or *Pistrinum*, of Modestus is one of the most interesting and well preserved. Four big mills of volcanic rock are still visible before the oven where 81 charred pieces of bread were found. Part of that bread is on exhibit in the Antiquarium.

34-HOUSE OF THE BEAR

 It takes its name from the mosaic in the entrance. At the back is a lovely fountain of colored mosaic

and seashells: against the delicate blue mosaic some exquisite figures stand out, including the *Swimming Venus,* small winged figures, little heads and a shoal of darting fish.

35-SITTIUS'INN

This modest lodging-house belonged to a certain Sittius. It had two entrances and displayed outside was a «for rent» sign offering a comfortable triclinium with three beds. Opposite is the *Lupanare,* the two storey house of prostitution, with small rooms adorned with erotic designs and drawings. At No. 47 in Vicolo del Lupa-

Stabian Baths - the courtyard of the paelestra.

nare is the house of Siricus, consisting of two connecting apartments with another entrance in Via Stabiana. They probably belonged to two rich merchants, Siricus and Nummianus, perhaps brothers or associates in the same business. The house on Vicolo del Lupanare was probably intended for commerce, for on the entrance floor we read: «*salve lucru(m)*» («business welcome»). In the triclinium there are paintings portraying *Neptune and Apollo, Drunken Hercules* and *Thetis with Vulcan*. In the section facing Via Stabiana the following are of interest: the Tuscan atrium, the marble impluvium, the fountain and the table supported by two «*trapezofori*». The triclinium is decorated with scenes of *cupids* and paintings of mythological subjects.

36-STABIAN BATHS

The entrance is on Via dell'Abbondanza. These baths date back to the times of the Roman colony. The building underwent numerous alterations in the course of time, especially the decorations which belong to the imperial period. After the 62 earthquake, restoration was begun, but was never completed because of the eruption. We enter a large palestra or gymnasium, with plastered columns on three sides; immediately to our left is the men's section of the vestibulum decorated with stucco; the ceiling has squares or losenges with war trophies and other

Stabian Baths - the "calidarium".
Opposite page: ***The Temple of Isis.***

designs. Those off to the *frigidarium* went through here and returned to the vestibule. It is circular, with a domed roof, and has decorations on the walls portraying sea fauna and shells.

Returning to the dressing-room, in the far left-hand corner is the entrance to the *tepidarium*, which was heated by hot air coming from beneath the floor. From here we enter lovely apsed room with a bathtub for ablutions: the *calidarium*. Note the lovely stucco frieze around the walls. To see the women's section we must return to the palestra and go back through the area we have already visited. Just outside the vestibule turn right, where, almost at the end of the colonnade, a passage leads to the dressing-room, the tepidarium and the calidarium. On the north side of the palestra is the oldest section of the baths which consisted of various small rooms with entrances on the Vicolo del Lupanare. The west side dates from the last period - notice the open-air swimming-pool flanked by dressing rooms and rooms for rubbing with oil and sana. These facilities were available to those participating in sports such as wrestling boxing and gymnastics.

37-HOUSE OF CORNELIUS RUFUS

Opposite the Stabian Baths is the House of Cornelius Rufus, which contains two beautiful «trapezofori» and an impluvium worthy of note. Next turn into Via Stabiana. Just after the intersection we find the **Temple of Jupiter Meilichios**, where - homage was paid to Zeus Meilichios, whose pre-Roman Greek cult was probably imported from Sicily. Note the beautiful tufo *altar*. Nearby is the **Temple of Isis**. Dating from pre-Roman times, it was reconstructed at the expense of Popidius Celsinus after the earthquake of 62. It is surrounded by high walls, and its original structure is well preserved.

Beside the staircase is a great altar; the tabernacle has a high podium with a *pronaos* and a small rectangular cella. In the corner of the peristyle to the southeast is a small temple, with stucco decorations, containing a tiny underground cellar in which water from the Nile was kept. Behind the temple is a large meeting-hall for the followers of Isis, and a short distance away the houses where the priests lived. After the Temple of Isis, continuing along the street, of the same name, we come to the **Samnite Gymnasium,** a small rectangular space defined on three sides by a Doric colonnade. It was built in the Samnite era by Vibius Vinicius, and was used by wealthy young Pompeians for sporting events.

The Triangular Forum - Entrance.

38-TRIANGULAR FORUM

The name comes from its geometrical shape, and here the Greek influence is more marked then anywhere else. One enters the **Triangular Forum** through the beautiful vestibule which consists of six Ionic columns (though only four are visible) with a public fountain in front. The extensive square is bounded on three sides by a portico composed of 95 Ionic columns. In front of the entrance is the pedestal on which a statue of Augustus' nephew, Claudius Marcellus, once stood. Almost in the center are remains of a **Doric temple** dedicated to the cult of Hercules and Minerva, all that is left from the period when Pompeii was under Etruscan rule.

39-GLADIATORS' BARRACKS

This grandiose quadruple portico originally was

Gladiator's Barracks - quadruple portico.

not for the gladiators. Instead, it was a meeting-place for the numerous spectators who crowded into the Large Theatre (which we will come to shortly). During pauses in the performances they used to stroll here, discussing what they had seen. In Nero's time it was converted into quarters for the gladiators taking part in the contests; they used to live here with their families and practise for the competitions. The living-area for the families spread over two floors of the four porticoes, and it was here that the fascinating weapons now on display in the Museo Archeologico in Naples were discovered.

40-LARGE THEATER

This attractive theater was constructed in accordance with Greek architectural techniques in the period between 200-150 B.C., and later enlarged by M. Artorius in the time of Augustus along purely Roman lines. The architect knew how to profit from the natural space offered by the hill, and there he constructed the «*cavea maxima*» bleachers reserved for the spectators (of which a few of the longer steps can be seen),

Large Theater - the "cavea" and the stage.
Opposite page, from the top: *Little Theater - the "cavea" and stage.*
Little Theater - the tufo rock telamon at the edge of the parapet.

large enough to accommodate five thousand people. The seating area was completely protected from the sun and rain by an enormous canopy (*velarium*) held up by poles fastened in rings that can still be seen at the back of the top seating area.

41-LITTLE THEATER

This was a covered theater for musical and prose per-

formances, and its capacity was not more then a thousand. It was built between 80 and 75 B. C. by magistrates G. Quintus Valgus and Marcus Porcius. Well-preserved in the «cavea maxima», it is one of the most beautiful examples of antique theatrical architecture extant. Going out into Via Stabiana we can see at the end the **Porta di Stabia**, one of the oldest city gates. Beyond the gate are a number of tombs.

House of Menander - peristyle.

42-HOUSE OF MENANDER

This is one of the loveliest and most interesting houses in Pompeii. It owes its name to a portrait of the Greek poet Menander. The house belonged to a patrician family, its owner was Quintus Poppeus. Here in 1930 archeologists brought to light a real treasure of silverware consisting of 115 pieces, now in the Naples archeological museum. The atrium has fourth style frescoes and a Lararium in the form of a small temple. The *exedra* to the left contains paintings of mythical subjects: *The Trojan Horse, The Death of Laocoon, The Meeting of Menelaus* and *Helen in Priam's Palace*. Then, after the tablinum, comes the grandiose

House of the Lovers - garden and peristyle.

peristyle with columns in red and black; to the north is the triclinium with two oeci. On the southern side is a series of rectangular apsed exedrae, with *portraits of Menander* and *hunting scenes*, and on the west side is a beautiful bathroom with a *calidarium* decorated with mosaics and pictures. From the bathroom a corridor leads to the kitchen and cellars. In one of these was the excavated set of silverware, placed here for safekeeping while the house was being restored. On the same block the **House of the Lovers**, is worthy of note: it has a skillfully decorated atrium, a peristyle with two rows of columns, and a garden. Near the luxuriously decorated portico is a small painting, with a Latin verse that reads: « amantes ut apes vitam mellitam exigunt» (Lovers, like bees, suck sweet life like honey).

43-HOUSE OF THE CITHARIST

No. 5 Via Stabiana, is the House of the Citharist, because a bronze statue of *Apollo the Citharist* (now in the archeological museum) was found here. An aristocratic dwelling from the Roman period, it was probably created by joining two houses (there are two atriums and three peristyles). The pictorial decoration has been moved to the archeological museum

44-HOUSE OF THE CRYPTOPORTICUS

The main interest here lies in the «*cryptoporticus*» which can be reached by descending a small flight of stairs with traces of second style decoration. The barrel vault is faced with stucco and decorated with floral motifs, and all round there is a large frieze with *Scenes from the Iliad*. Here in

House of Cryptoporticus - details of stucco and painted decorations.

House of Lucius Ceius Secundus.

Fullonica of Stephani.

special cases are plaster casts of those who sought refuge from the eruption in the cryptoporticus (they died of asphyxiation). In the triclinium are second style decorations, with caryatids, small pictures and still lifes. On the same block is the **House of Lucius Ceius Secundus**, with a beautiful stucco façade. Beyond the vestibule are casts of two doors and a restored painted ceiling. From the tetrastyle atrium a small staircase leads up to the second floor, where there is a model of a cupboard. On the garden walls are frescoes revealing Egyptian influence. Next is the **Fullonica of Stephani**, a house converted into a laundry, with all its equipment. To the right of the atrium is the lovely **House of the Lararium**. On its roof is a frieze on a blue ground with episodes from the last book of the Iliad.

45-HOUSE OF PAQUIUS PROCULUS

That the owner was an influential personage, we know from the fact that his name recurs in various electoral programs. In

Museo Archeologico, Naples - Portrait of Paquius Proculus and his wife.

House of the Ephebe - the open-air triclinium.

the vestibule is a picture of a chained dog. The tablinum and triclinium are adorned with beautiful mosaics. The skeletons of seven children hidden during the eruption were discovered in an exedra on the north side of the peristyle. Next door is the **House of the Ephebe**, so called because a statue in bronze of an *Ephebe* was found here (now in the archeological museum). The complex is made up of three apartments joined together. Particularly worthy of note are the triclinium with couches and a marble inlay floor, and, in the garden, the Lararium and a painting of *Mars and Venus*. Now, we shall glance briefly into the **House of the Priest Amandus**, No. 7 on Via dell'Abbondanza. There is an interesting triclinium with third style paintings of *Polyphemos and Galatea, Perseus and Andromeda, Hercules in the Garden of the Hesperides* and *Dedalus and Icarus*.

Thermopolium of Asellina - the serving counter.

46-THE VERECUNDUS WORKSHOP

This is one of the most typical of the Pompeii factories. Here dress materials and felt objects were produced and clothes manufactured. It has a nice façade with a protruding roof. Beside the entrance are four paintings. Two are dedicated to gods considered the factory's protectors: *Mercury and Venus of Pompeii in a chariot drawn by four elephants*. On the right are scenes of the factory in operation and selling over the counter.

47-REFECTORIES AND THERMOPOLIUM OF ASELLINA

Two long open galleries formed by columns and pillars were used as dining halls. Originally they served as textile factories and their proprietors' dwellings. Next door is the **Thermopolium of Asellina**, a direct ancestor of the modern bar, where hot and cold drinks were sold. Skilful excavation has unearthed it in its entirety, complete with terracotta and bronze

Via dell'Abbondanza.

crockery. Notice the oil-lamp hanging from the ceiling, the urn for drinks and the small board with round notches in varying sizes in which the money received from clients was kept. Outside the thermopolium we see women's names, Asellina, Aegle, Maria and Smyrna: we can assume that the clients were not insensible to the charms of these girls, probably workers in the shop and the tavern on the second floor. Leaving the Thermopolium of Asellina, after a block we come to the **House of Caius Julius Polibius**. Originally built in the Samnite period, it underwent various alterations for commercial reasons. Nevertheless it is interesting to read the poem scratched by a melancholy poet on the side wall. Translated it reads: «Nothing in the world can endure forever. Now the sun shines clearly, now it sinks into the ocean. The moon, half-gone, shortly before appeared full... Thus, every feather obeys the wind, the most cruel denial of love».

Opposite the House of Polibius

House of Trebius Valens - the outdoor triclinium.

on Via dell'Abbondanza, are the latest excavations. At No. 1 is the aristocratic **House of the Beautiful Impluvium**, entered through a shop. After the earthquake it was being restored. Particularly admirable are the atrium and the tablinum; in the former the marble impluvium has mosaic decorations, and in the latter are third style wall decorations on a blue ground. No. 3 is the **House of Successus**, where, in a cubiculum to the left of the atrium, is a mural representing a *Frightened putto being attacked by a duck*. On the painting is inscribed «Successus»; from whence came the name of the house. Under the small portico in the garden is a statuette of a nude youth with a dove used as a trapezoforum. At No.5 is the

House of the Orchard, which one enters through a shop. It was called «of the Orchard» since the cubiculae contain paintings of fruit trees. The originals probably once grew in the owner's «horti pompeiani».

48-HOUSE OF TREBIUS VALENS

Before World War II this house was famous because the façade was completely covered with inscriptions about elections, performances at the amphitheater, the names of the impresarios of the various champions of the gladiatorial games, eulogies on the

House of the Moralist - the triclinium.

champions themselves, and the like. Today almost nothing remains of these inscriptions, which were destroyed during the war. The interior of the house is quite interesting. It has a striking checker pattern adorning the peristyle, an out-door triclinium under an arbour where water spouts, and a beautiful cubiculum with the second style paintings.

49-SCHOLA ARMATURARUM

This large area was the base for a good-sized military organization, and this fact dictated the style of decoration. On the outside pilasters are trophies of war, and on those inside is the recurrent motif of stylized candelabra surmounted by military emblems. From impressions on the wall it can easily be seen that between the pillars there was a series of partitions where training weapons and show pieces were kept. At the end of the neighboring lane is the **House of Pinarius Cerialis**, probably the home of a skilled artist, expert in the art of engraving and carving precious stones, ivory and cameos, for in his house 114 stones, both cut and uncut were found. The two-storey house has a theatrical scene from the tragedy *Iphigenia at Taurus* in the garden portico.

Returning to Via dell'Abbondanza, next to a tavern, Nos. 2-3

House of Loreius Tiburtinus - frescoes on the fountain wall.

are two connecting houses which belonged to T. Arrius Polites and M. Epidus Hymenaeus, who probably were related. The house of the latter is known as the **House of the Moralist** because of three paintings in the triclinium, situated under an open gallery of the floor above. Lettered in white on a black ground were precepts which the owner of the house wished to be observed: 1) «The servant shall wash and dry the feet of the host; a cloth must protect the cushions (of the bed) and our linen must be well cared for. 2) Abandon lascivious looks, and do not cast sweet glances at the women of others; be chaste in speech. 3) Abstain from anger if you can, if not return to your own home».

50-HOUSE OF LOREIUS TIBURTINUS

 This patrician house has a large doorway with brass studs by which we enter the rectangular atrium elaborately decorated on a ground of red, white and yellow. Beyond the atrium and the peri-

House of Loreius Tiburtinus - the garden with the transverse canal.

style there is a loggia or long open gallery, and a portico with a pergola, in the center of which is a small tetrastyle temple. Then there is a pool bordered by marble statues with motifs of animals and Muses, and, at the end, is the triclinium with two signed paintings (Lucius pinxit) representing *Narcissus* and *Pyramus and Thisbe*. On the other side of the loggia is another triclinium decorated with a frieze of *Scenes from the Iliad* and *Episodes from the legend of Heracles*. On the west side is a cubiculum which gives us one of the most perfect examples of the fourth style painting on a white background. Amongst the various figures and medallions note the *figure of a priest of the cult of Isis* with an inscription (*amplus alumnus Tiburs*) which has been identified as a portrait of one of the members of the patrician family.

House of Venus - peristyle.

51-HOUSE OF VENUS

The name derives from a monumental mural painting at the end of the garden found in 1952. Showing *Venus on a great seashell escorted by cupids*, it cannot be described as a masterpiece, but the artist did managed to create a naturalistic and colorful effect all the same. On the left is an image of *Mars*, and, in a cubiculum on the right side of the atrium, there is a medallion with *Young Citharist* and a *still life*, on a white background.

House of Venus - Venus on the shell.

House of Venus - Mars.

House of Julia Felix - the portico and fish-pond.

52-HOUSE OF JULIA FELIX

This house covers the a whole block and although it was first excavated in 1755-1757, the excavations went on until 1952-1953. The name of the proprietress was easily discovered because on one of the entrance doors was a «For Rent» sign which mentioned her name (it is now in the archeological museum). This very large complex is made up of three parts: the house of the owner on Via dell'Abbondanza, and on the same road a public bath, a tavern and area for rent. In the eighteenth century the building was pillaged, for example the nine figures of *Apollo and the Muses*, now in the Louvre in Paris, were looted from a room in the northeast wing. It must have had a beautiful garden, its colonnade and fishpond (*euripus*) decorated with sculptures in marble and terracotta. A fine terracotta representing

House of Julia Felix - terracotta statue of the Greek sage, Pittacos.

the Greek sage *Pittacos* is extant. Under the western portico is the triclinium, which was decorated with a *still life* frieze now in the archeological museum. The bathroom has more or less the same features as those we have already seen, with a dressing room, rectangular *frigidarium, tepidarium* and *laconicum* with a dome, here only used for Turkish baths. At the end of this street is the *Porta di Sarno*.

Amphitheater - exterior view.

53-AMPHITHEATER

The building was constructed in 80 B.C. by the same builders responsible for the Little Theater, and it can be considered as the oldest amphitheater which has come down to us. The impressive elliptical building, with its giant bleachers could hold 12,000 spectators; it is 135 by 104 meters. At the top of the steps are great rings of stone which were used to support the frame of the «*velarium*», a type of awning spread out over the spectators to protect them from the sun or the rain. There are no underground rooms.

54-THE GREAT PALESTRA

Opposite the amphitheater is the **Great Palestra** (gymnasium) which was excavated between 1936 and 1951. It comprises a rectangular space bounded on three sides by porticoes, with a large swimming pool in the center. Here the young Pompeians used to come and train for athletic games in their chosen sports. The area is 130 by 140 meters, and the pool was surrounded by two rows of large plane-trees which provided relief from the heat and the sun.

Above: *Amphitheater - inside*. Below: ***The Great Palestra.***

Orchard of the Fugitives - casts of victims of the eruption.

55-ORCHARD OF THE FUGITIVES AND THE PORTA DI NOCERA

If you have time, go from the Palestra to the nearby Vicolo di Castricio. Here new excavations have brought to light shops and houses. Amongst the most important of these discoveries are the **Officina del Garum** where a renowned sauce, known as *garum*, was prepared from salt-water and fish entrails, and the **Thermopolium of the Phoenix** which had a truckgarden and grapevines on pergolas. On the right-hand block at the corner of Via Nocera is the **House of the Lararium of Sarnus**, a modest

Porta di Nocera.

house which tells us how maritime business was conducted in Pompeii. The lararium in the courtyard is in the form of a small temple, with a painting in popular style showing the loading of farm products onto a small boat. Farther on is the **House of the Arches**, a lovely house where in the garden portico is the motif of an arch built on columns. Going back, 6 Via di Nocera, on the last block on the right before the fortification walls, is the **Orchard of the Fugitives**, discovered in 1961 behind the portico of a rustic house with an orchard. Here, in the ashes, were the remains of thirteen victims of the eruption. When you turn round you will see the **Porta di Nocera**, built before Roman times, and later restored by the Romans. Outside the gate, along the fortification wall are casts of the victims found in the neighborhood. Beyond is the **Necropolis**, excavated a short time ago.

Via dei Sepolcri.

SUBURBAN VILLAS

56 - VILLA OF DIOMEDES

A visit to the excavations at Pompeii would not be complete without seeing the Villa of Diomedes and the famous Villa of the Mysteries. They can be reached by car or cab, or on foot (just under a kilometer from Porta Ercolano). Beyond Porta Ercolano is *Via dei Sepolcri,* which was unearthed between 1763 and 1938. It is a road about half a kilometer long flanked by beautiful sepulchres from Greek and Roman times, but also dotted with taverns and villas. The effect it

makes is singular; the variety of architectural forms of the patrician homes, porticoes and villas leave a memorable impression. The brevity of this guide precludes our stopping as we ought, in the various burial-grounds, so we shall pass through on our way to the **Villa of Diomedes**. This majestic suburban dwelling came to light in 1771-1774, when it evoked considerable interest because of the discovery, in an underground portico, of eighteen victims of the eruption. Hardly anything remains of its sumptuous decorations, some of which can be found in the archeological museum. However, it is fascinating to explore as we can get an idea of the lay-out of an aristocratic villa built outside city limits. The complex appears to have been carefully planned so that

A chapel-shaped tomb; below: *tomb with pillared edicula.*

Tomb of the Married Couple.

Villa of Diomedes. Opposite page: *Villa of the Mysteries.*

the inhabitants could enjoy lovely views from both inside and out. For this reason it faces west and has two recessed floors. The building is laid out around an atrium-peristyle and protrudes into the enormous garden on the ground level. Above the arcades, which surrounded all of the «*viridarium*», ran a «*solarium*» and an «*ambulatio*», terrace where people could walk and take sun. At either end there were two towers from which the sea view could be enjoyed under the protection of a roof. Below the arcade ran a huge gallery (cryptoporticus) which underwent constant alterations so it could accommodate amphoras for wine, in accordance with the needs of its last owner, certainly a prominent wine merchant. We exit the excavated area by going through the custodian's house that opens directly onto the avenue of the Villa of the Mysteries.

57-VILLA OF THE MYSTERIES

We find ourselves before a massive square building, which consists of some sixty rooms in all. The grandiose **Villa of the Mysteries** is so called because one of the rooms has fresco master-pieces which portray (it is thought), *the initiation of brides to the Dionysiac mysteries.* The villa was discovered in 1902, excavated between 1909-1910, and almost entirely restored between 1929 and 1930. Here we find, collected from different sour-ces, all the functional, architectural and decorative elements of Pom-peian life. We are indebted to Professor of Archeology Amedeo Maiuri for his most detailed descrip-tions of this extraordinary and mon-umental building (and especially

107

Villa of the Mysteries - Decorations on a black background.

painting, of which he made a profound critical study, and published an indispensable reference book for scholars). A complete description of the Villa would take many pages, so we shall limit ourselves just to a visit to the famous hall of painting. From a large semi-circular exedra with windows flanked by roof-gardens, we go straight into the original *tablinum*, which was converted into an ordinary room. Here note the beautiful miniature wall decora-

tions on a black background in the Egyptian style. From the tablinum one enters the cubiculum containing second style paintings, amongst which should be noted the figure of the *Dancing Satyr*. Then we go through a small door into the room with the most paintings. If it is your first visit you will be overwhelmed by the magnificent scene on the wall. You will be captivated by the peculiar mystical atmosphere. The whole is permeated with a sense of

Villa of the Mysteries - Dancing satyr.

*Villa of the Mysteries - Cupid admiring the bride, detail from the scenes of the
Dionysiac Mysteries.*

Villa of the Mysteries - Flagellation of the initiate and the dance of the new initiate.

Villa of the Mysteries - The sacrificing priestess and an attendant.

mysterious meditation, notwithstanding the fact that the subject is unrelated to religious orders as we know them today. There is a controversy as to the meaning of the composition. Nevertheless, as we said before, the prevalent opinion is that it portrays *the initiation of brides to the Dionysiac mysteries.* The cult of Dionysius was widespread throughout Campania and Etruria, and even reached Rome, but its orgiastic and obscene character provoked severe sanctions by the Senate. For this reason the cult was practised in private only by a few initiates. At the Villa of the Mysteries the «domina», or lady of the house, was an initiate or priestess of the Dionysiac rites, which she celebrated in the utmost secrecy in this triclinium. She commissioned a Campanian artist who lived about the middle of the first century B. C. to paint this remarkable composition, in the second style. The scenes along the walls are peopled with 29 life-size figures, divided into groups, each of which is participating in one of the sacred or profane moments of the Dionysiac rites. The pictures

Villa of the Mysteries - Detail of the Marriage of Dionysius and Ariadne.

shoud be viewed from left to right: 1) *Initiation with the reading of the ritual by a young boy;* 2) *The sacred agape, with a young girl holding a dish with offering;* 3) *Silenus playing his lyre, and a pastoral scene;* 4) *Terrified woman fleeing from the sight of a demon lashing her companion;* 5) *Silenus with Satyrs;* 6) *The Marriage of Dionysius and Ariadne;* 7) *Bacchante kneeling in the act of lifting a drape which covers the symbol of peace and fertility;* 8) *Woman scourged, and a nude female Bacchante dancing, as overcome by mysticism;* 9) *Toilet of a bride preparing herself for initiation to the Mysteries;* 10) *Woman sitting draped in a mantle* - this is probably a portrait of the lady of the house, the priestess of Dionysius. The great frieze, designed to unfold along a single plane, betrays the hand of a great artist who knew how to create a monumental effect. The figures are placed on a deep red background against which bright yellows, greens, and purples stand out. The groups are articulated in a rhythmical treatment worthy of a great painter of the classic era, so much so that it is probable that this artist must have been influenced somehow by classical art. His skill in the use of line and color is such that this work must be considered one of the great masterpieces of Antiquity.

Villa of the Mysteries - Detail of the reading from the Ritual of the Dionysiac Mysteries.

Villa of the Mysteries - Silenus playing the lyre, pastoral scene and the terrified initiate fleeing in terror as her companion is whipped.

Excavations on the road to New Pompeii.

NEW POMPEII

Leaving the excavations by the Amphitheater entrance, on the left is the beginning of the built-up area of new Pompeii. It is actually a small town occupying an area inhabited even after the famous eruption of 79 A.D. Called **Campo Pompeiano**, it has undergone many vicissitudes during the past centuries. A church dedicated to the Saviour was built there, as well as a castle which belonged to Caracciolo. The whole area was feudal territory which was passed from hand to hand, changing with the political situation of the Kingdom of Naples. In 1873 the lawyer Bartolo Longo (1841-1926), a religious and charitable man, founded the **Sanctuary of the Madonna of the Rosary**, around which, with the help of the faithful, he built charitable institutions and orphanages. The sanctuary soon became a center of fervent worship.

Many pilgrims from all over Italy flock here, especially in summer and autumn. In the main square is the imposing sanctuary designed by the architect Antonio Cua. It was begun on May 8, 1876, consecrated on May 7, 1891, and enlarged 1933-1939 (by the engineer Spirito Chiappetta). The façade was designed by Giovanni Rispoli, who conceived it in two architectural orders: the longer

New Pompeii - Museo Vesuviano, exterior;
below: **Monument to Bartolo Longo.**

Detail of the monument to Bartolo Longo.

Ionic, and the upper Corinthian. Above the middle of the papal loggia (the sanctuary bears the title of Basilica, and the Rector Archbishop is appointed by the Pope) is the marble statue of the *Madonna of the Rosary* by the sculptor Gaetano Chiaramonte. By the façade is the *bell-tower* constructed between 1912 and 1925 by the architect Aristide Lenori. It is 80 meters high, consisting of five floors reached through a lovely bronze door. At the corners of the third floor are four bronze *angels*, and a belfry with eleven bells. In a niche on the fourth floor is a gigantic statue of the *Sacred Heart of Jesus*, and at the top is a terrace surmounted by a large cross. From the terrace (which can be reached by a lift) there is a superb view— one can see old and new Pompeii, Vesuvius, the sea, the Sarno valley and the mountains beyond. The interior of the sanctuary is filled with precious marble creating a highly colored effect; in the dome there are frescoes, and on the walls mosaics. In the middle is the main altar with the venerated image of the *Virgin of the Rosary* surrounded by myriads of precious stones. It is worthwhile to visit the *Treasury*, entered from the left aisle, vaunting precious religious fittings. There is a painting, a *Saint Paul* attributed to Fra Bartolomeo, a *candelabra for Easter candles* by Vincenzo Ierace, as well as portraits of Popes, benefactors and founders. The square communicates with the square of the City Hall; to the left is the Via Sacra. Here are the «**Terme Fonte Salutare**», which with mudbaths, offers effective remedies for rheumatism, asthenia, exhaustion, metabolic disorders and other diseases.

Sanctuary of the Madonna of the Rosary.

Sanctuary of the Madonna of the Rosary - detail of the frescoes on the dome.

Sanctuary of the Madonna of the Rosary - Above: ***Bartolo Longo offers the Sanctuary to Pope Leo XIII;*** below: *the main altar with the venerated image of the Virgin.*

USEFUL INFORMATION

•**Azienda Autonoma di Cura, Soggiorno e Turismo**
Via Sacra, 1 - Pompei ☎ 081.850.72.55/850.84.51 **Fax** 081.863.24.01

HOURS FOR VISITING THE EXCAVATIONS:

The excavations are open daily from 9:00 a.m. until one hour before sunset, but you may remain on the grounds for one hour after closing time.

From 2/Jan. to 15/ Jan. until: 3:00 p.m. - from 16/Jan. to 31/Jan. until:: 3:20 p.m.
From 1/Feb. to 15/ Feb. until: 3:40 p.m. - from 16/Feb. to 29/Feb. until: 4:00 p.m.
From 1/Mar. to 15 Mar. until: 4:20 p.m. - from 16/Mar. to 31/Mar. until 4:40 p.m.
From 1/Apr. to 15/Apr. until: 6:00 p.m. - from 16/Apr. to 30/Apr. until: 6:30 p.m.
From 1/May to 15/May until: 6:30 p.m. - from 16/May to 31/May until: 6:45 p.m.
From 1/Jun. to 15/Aug. until: 7:00 p.m. - from 16/Aug. to 31/Aug. until: 6:40 p.m.
From 1/Sep. to 15/Sep. until: 6:20 p.m. - from 16/Sep. to 30/Sep. until: 4:40 p.m.
From 1/Oct. to 15/Oct. until: 3:40 p.m. - from 16/Oct. to 31/Oct. until: 3:15 p.m.
From 1/Nov. to 15/Nov.until: 3:00 p.m. - from 16/Nov. to 31/Dec. until: 2:45 p.m.

The excavations are closed on 1 January, 1 May and 25 December.

HOTELS

***

Bristol, p.zza Vittorio Veneto 1/3 (historic center)... ☎ 081.850.30.05
fax 081.863.16.25
Del Santuario, p.zza Longo............................. ☎ 081.850.61.65
fax 081.850.28.22
Del Sole, via Plinio, 15/21 (historic center)........... ☎ 081.863.17.00
fax 081.863.17.00
Diomede, via Mazzini, 46 (historic center)...... ☎ 081.850.75.86
fax 081.863.15.20
Forum, via Roma, 99 (historic center)........... ☎ 081.850.11.70
fax 081.850.61.32
Giovanna, via Acqua Salsa, 12......................... ☎ 081.850.61.61
fax 081.850.73.23
Palma, via Piave, 15 (historic center)........... ☎ 081.863.11.68
fax 081.850.18.05
Villa Laura, via Delle Salle, 13 (historic center)... ☎ 081.863.10.24
**
fax 081.850.48.93
Amitrano, via Lepanto, 93............................. ☎ 081.863.10.89
fax 081.850.52.33
Amleto, via Longo, 4................................... ☎ 081.863.10.04

HOTELS

Astoria, viale Mazzini, 65.................................. ☎ 081.863.10.74
Bristol Snc., p.zza Vittorio Veneto 1/3................ ☎ 081.863.16.25
Calypso, via Mazzini, 93 (historic center)...... ☎ 081.850.54.45
fax 081.850.43.90
Europa, p.zza Santuario, 30 (historic center)... ☎ 081.863.21.90
fax 081.863.33.42
Villa dei Misteri, via Villa dei Misteri, 11 ☎ 081.861.35.93
(200 m. from the excavations) fax 081.862.29.83
Vittoria, Pompei Scavi.................................. ☎ 081.536.81.66
fax 081.862.35.77

*

Apollo, via C. Alberto, 18................................. ☎ 081.863.03.09
Due Pini, via San Giuseppe, 62....................... ☎ 081.863.19.25
Miele, via C. Alberto, 44 (Sanctuary M. of the Rosary) ☎ 081.863.12.79

RESTAURANTS

Bar Tiberius Snc., via Villa dei Misteri, 1/b............ ☎ 081.861.35.50
Il Principe, p.zza Longo, 8 (historic center)...... ☎ 081.850.55.66
Marius et Caesar S.a.s., via Plinio, 52................. ☎ 081.861.09.67
M.E.C. da Andrea, via Plinio, 45 (near the excavations) ☎ 081.536.34.98
Hostaria del Gallo Nero, via Mazzini, 116/118........ ☎ 081.863.00.34
Osteria da Peppino, via Duca d'Aosta, 37............ ☎ 081.850.48.21
Palma, p.zza V. Veneto, 2 (historic center)...... ☎ 081.863.28.75
President, p.zza Schettini, 12/13 (historic center)... ☎ 081.850.72.45
Suisse, p.zza Portamarina (near the excavations) ☎ 081.861.01.85
Vesuvio, via Plinio, 123.................................. ☎ 081.536.74.94
Zì Caterina, Via Roma, 20 (historic center)...... ☎ 081.850.74.47

PIZZERIAS

Carlo Alberto, via Carlo Alberto, 15.................. ☎ 081.863.32.31
Catapano Valeria, via Astolelle, 24.................... ☎ 081.863.81.95
Il Diavoletto, via Nolana, 5............................. ☎ 081.863.78.32
Lucullus, via Bottaro (c/o Città Mercato).............. ☎ 081.536.99.32

CAMPSITES

Camping Pompei, via Plinio.......................... ☎ 081.862.28.82
Camping Spartacus Bungalow, via Plinio............ ☎ 081.536.95.19
Camping Zeus, via Villa dei Misteri.................. ☎ 081.861.53.20

INDEX